Trumpeter Swan

Families

Hello Friends!

**This picture book is about
Trumpeter Swan families
who chose to spend time at a
particular pond,
HERON POND,
located at the
Riverlands Migratory Bird
Sanctuary in
West Alton, Missouri.**

**These pictures were taken
between
December 2012
and
January 2018.**

Here's a family of seven flying in.
I wonder why the one in the back is trailing behind
and hope he catches up!

It looks like he is catching up. There are REALLY six in the front group.
They are flying very closely so it's hard to tell them apart.

**Ahhhh. Feet coming down and wings are down too.
They will be landing very soon.**

Closer and closer. Wings changed again.

Almost there.

Home at last! There are other families already there.

Heron Pond is not really a pond, it's actually a field of about 89 acres. In the fall and winter there is water in the pond about a yard deep and in the spring and summer there's not much water, it's more like a shallow wetland then.
The Mississippi River is on the other side of the road!

Usually swans live in family groups. This is a family of four.
Here, as you can see, others share the space.

Children
Adult
Adult

Young swans are called cygnets. They keep this gray brown coloring until they are about one year old.

They can really move their necks around.

The swans have a lot to do while they appear to be
lounging around on the pond.
This swan is "fluffing" her feathers. They do that to help
separate their feathers in preparation for groomng.

They are grooming. Trumpeter Swans have a lot of
feathers to take care of. About 24,000 actually!!

There is always eating to be done.
Here she is eating plants under the water.
This includes seeds, leaves and roots.
Their long necks can reach way down, almost a yard.

She's found something.

Sometimes
they
dive in head
first
looking for
that tasty
meal.

There must be
something
good
down there.

He's landing. Look at his feet.
They seem very big.

It appears that the foot length is one fifth the wing length, doesn't it?

She is stretching out her wing.

27
Are there 27 feathers here? What do you think?
1
23

Sometimes the children wander off a little bit.

Sometimes the adults like to visit together
by themselves too.

But often there is a lot of babysitting.

One of the adults has a yellow band on.
Trumpeter Swans sometimes get banded
so they can be tracked for migration purposes.

When Trumpeter Swans are planning to take off and go somewhere else,
they discuss it loudly and in swan language.
Their heads bend up and down several times for a few minutes.
When they finally agree on what to do, they take off.

Heads curving down.

Definitely chatting.

You can almost hear them from here!

They have decided.

They are starting the flying process. They need 100 yards to take off.

They're on their way!

CATS

Cats
Lexi my Cat
Cat Portraits
CATS SPEAK
Text by
Linda Whitefeather

DOGS

Dogs of Circle Lake
Dog Portraits
Barnhunt
Seasoned Dogs
With Bright Shiny Faces

Variety

Go Fish!
What Are they Thinking?
What's A Family Anyway?
Animals Don't Wear
Lipstick
Subliminal Nuances of
Animal Behavior

Coloring Books

Tra La La
Time to Smell the Flowers
A-Z-Capital Letters
a-z- lower case letters

Bonobo Books

I'm Lucy:
A Day in the Life
of a Young Bonobo.
(Text by Mathea Levine and
Afterword by Jane Goodall)

Is Lucy Singing?
Grooming Bonobos:
Lucy Loves it.
Growing up Bonobo
Bonobo Lucy Grows Up
Bonobo Lucy and
her Baby Yuli

Books on Empathy
using Bonobo pictures.

Insides Out
You Scared Me
I'm Different-You're Different
Teacher's Manual
(Written by Anne Paris)

That's it so far!